Contents

SKELTON NEWBY HALL (
SKELTON-ON-URE
RIPON
HG4 5AF

Name: _____

sh ch

Practise these letter joins by writing the words
in the box.

Think about this! Remember to Look, Say, Cover,
Write and Check!
When you have finished, write each word
three more times on another sheet of paper.

> clash hush shall sheet shell show
> slosh wish chat chest chick chin
> inch itch much pinch

Write all of the words that have the *sh* letter join.

_____

_____

_____

_____

_____

Write all of the words that have the *ch* letter join.

_____

_____

_____

_____

2 Letter joins

wh th

Practise these letter joins by writing the words in the box.

Think about this!

Remember to Look, Say, Cover, Write and Check!
When you have finished, write each word three more times on another sheet of paper.

> *whale wheel when where which*
> *whiff who why bath moth myth*
> *path thank thin thing think*

Write all of the words that have the *wh* letter join.

_____

_____

_____

_____

_____

_____

Write all of the words that have the *th* letter join.

_____

_____

_____

_____

_____

_____

3 Letter joins

bl cl gl

Practise these letter joins by writing the words
in the box.

Think about this! Remember to Look, Say, Cover, Write and Check!
When you have finished, write each word three more times on another sheet of paper.

bland blip blow blue class cliff clip clue gland glass gleam glow

Write all of the words that have the *bl* letter join.

Write all of the words that have the *cl* letter join.

Write all of the words that have the *gl* letter join.

(4) Letter joins

cr dr tr

Practise these letter joins by writing the words
in the box.

Think about this! Remember to Look, Say, Cover,
Write and Check!
When you have finished, write each word
three more times on another sheet of paper.

*crash crop cross crust drip drop
drum drunk trip true trunk trust*

Write all of the words that have the *cr* letter join.

_____

_____

Write all of the words that have the *dr* letter join.

_____

_____

Write all of the words that have the *tr* letter join.

_____

_____

5 Letter joins

sm sn sp

Practise these letter joins by writing the words in the box.

small smell smile smoke snake snap sniff snip spell spill spin spun

Write all of the words that have the *sm* letter join.

_____

_____

Write all of the words that have the *sn* letter join.

_____

_____

Write all of the words that have the *sp* letter join.

_____

_____

cl   sl

Practise these letter joins by writing the words
in the box.

Think about this!   Remember to Look, Say, Cover,
Write and Check!
When you have finished, write each word
three more times on another sheet of paper.

*clan clank clear click clock cluck
slam sleep slid slim sling slink*

Write all of the words that have the *cl* letter join.

_____

_____

_____

_____

_____

Write all of the words that have the *sl* letter join.

_____

_____

_____

_____

_____

7 Initial letters

Add the days of the week to the reminder list below, in the correct order, and think of something you might need to remember on each day.
Make sure to use capitals for the initial letters only.

Monday Thursday Sunday Tuesday
Saturday Wednesday Friday

Week beginning	Things to remember

Initial letters

Add the months of the year to the boxes below,
choosing a box of the right width for each word.
Make sure to use capitals for the initial letters only.

April November February September
January May December March July
October June August

Colour seven of the eight borders in the wheel,
then write the correct colour name in each segment.
Make sure to use capitals for the intitial letters only.
Which segment has a name but doesn't need
to be coloured?

Red Yellow Blue Green Black Purple
Orange White

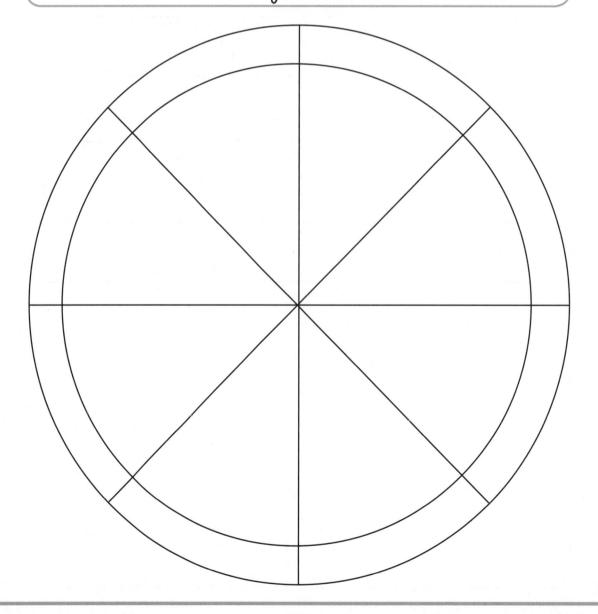

Write a school subject name in the centre of each of the notebook labels. Make sure to use capitals for the initial letters only. Which labels should the longer subject names go on?

Reading Writing Numeracy History
P.E. Geography Science Art Music

11 Putting words in signs

Street names on signs are almost always printed in capital letters. Complete the street name signs below.

ROAD AVENUE CRESCENT PLACE
STREET SQUARE WAY

RATHBONE _____

MORNINGTON _____

SEBASTOPOL _____

HOPE _____

WINDERMERE _____

MANDELA _____

BLACKPOOL _____

Now make a sign for the street you live in.

_____

 **12** **Putting words in signs**

Printing words in capital letters and adding exclamation marks help to give signs more importance.
Add the words in the box to the signs.

Think about this! Print each word carefully.
Think about which words will need long sign boxes and which will fit into short sign boxes.
Remember to add the exclamation marks!

DANGER!   STOP!   PLEASE WALK   FIRE EXIT
OPEN   CLOSED   CLASS 3C   ROOM 4

Use the example addresses below to help you write your own name and address and the name and address of your school.

Gemma Smith
35, Boomtown Road
Thistletown
Wessex SD3 Q32

Woodfield School
Any Road
Any Town
Anyshire AT39 6KK

Write your name and address.

_____

_____

_____

_____

Now write the name and address of your school.

_____

_____

_____

_____

Number-words

Write each of the following number-words
on the correct line.

Think about this! Read each number-word aloud as you write it. Practise writing each word three more times on another sheet of lined paper. Remember to Look, Say, Cover, Write and Check!

> Nine Two Ten Four One Six
> Three Five Eight Seven

1 _____   6 _____

2 _____   7 _____

3 _____   8 _____

4 _____   9 _____

5 _____   10 _____

(15) Number-words

Write each of the following number-words
on the correct line.

Think about this! Read each number-word aloud as you write it. Practise writing each word three more times on another sheet of lined paper. Remember to Look, Say, Cover, Write and Check!

> Nineteen Twelve Twenty Fourteen
> Eleven Sixteen Eighteen Thirteen
> Fifteen Seventeen

11 _____   16 _____

12 _____   17 _____

13 _____   18 _____

14 _____   19 _____

15 _____   20 _____

wh bl tr

Practise writing all of the words from activity 2 that have the *wh* letter join.

_____

_____

_____

_____

Practise writing all of the words from activity 3 that have the *bl* letter join.

_____

_____

_____

_____

Practise writing all of the words from activity 4 that have the *tr* letter join.

_____

_____

_____

_____

Handwriting check 1:
"The Alligator"

Write this poem in your best handwriting.

The alligator chased his tail
Which hit him on the snout;
He nibbled, gobbled, swallowed it,
And turned right inside-out.

Mary MacDonald

ake ike oke

Practise writing each of the words in the box.

bake cake make snake bike like mike trike coke joke poke woke

Think about this! Say each word aloud as you write it. Remember to Look, Say, Cover, Write and Check! When you have finished, write each word three more times on another sheet of paper.

ade ide ode

Practise writing each of the words in the box.

> *blade glade shade trade bride side tide*
> *wide code mode rode strode*

Think about this!
Say each word aloud as you write it.
Remember to Look, Say, Cover,
Write and Check!
When you have finished, write each word
three more times on another sheet of paper.

_____

_____

_____

_____

_____

_____

_____

_____

20 Word practice

ate ite ute

Practise writing each of the words in the box.

grate late mate state bite quite white write brute cute flute mute

Think about this!

Say each word aloud as you write it.
Remember to Look, Say, Cover,
Write and Check!
When you have finished, write each word
three more times on another sheet of paper.

Word practice

ai ay

Practise writing each of the words in the box.

nail rain snail trail train wait clay
day play pray spray stray

Think about this!

Say each word aloud as you write it.
Remember to Look, Say, Cover,
Write and Check!
When you have finished, write each word
three more times on another sheet of paper.

22 Word practice

eigh ea ey a aigh

Practise writing each of the words in the box.

> *eight freight weigh break great steak*
> *grey obey they apron gravy straight*

Think about this!

Say each word aloud as you write it.
Remember to Look, Say, Cover,
Write and Check!
When you have finished, write each word
three more times on another sheet of paper.

_ _

_ _

_ _

_ _

_ _

23 Word practice

ee ea e-e

Practise writing each of the words in the box.

> bee knees seed seem beach dream
> leaf read here scheme theme these

Think about this!

Say each word aloud as you write it.
Remember to Look, Say, Cover,
Write and Check!
When you have finished, write each word
three more times on another sheet of paper.

24 Word practice

ie ey e

Practise writing each of the words in the box.

> *believe field niece relieve donkey key*
> *money because depend equal me*

Think about this!

Say each word aloud as you write it.
Remember to Look, Say, Cover,
Write and Check!
When you have finished, write each word
three more times on another sheet of paper.

_____

_____

_____

_____

_____

_____

25

25 Word practice

i-e igh

Practise writing each of the words in the box.

fine grime knife nice ride stile bright
fight flight right sigh sight

Think about this!

Say each word aloud as you write it.
Remember to Look, Say, Cover,
Write and Check!
When you have finished, write each word
three more times on another sheet of paper.

26 Word practice

ie y ye

Practise writing each of the words in the box.

die fried lie tie by fry my sty bye dye eye rye

Think about this!

Say each word aloud as you write it.
Remember to Look, Say, Cover,
Write and Check!
When you have finished, write each word
three more times on another sheet of paper.

Practice page 2

ode ai ee igh

Practise writing all of the words from activity 19 that have the *ode* letter join.

_____

_____

Practise writing all of the words from activity 21 that have the *ai* letter join.

_____

_____

Practise writing all of the words from activity 23 that have the *ee* letter join.

_____

_____

Practise writing all of the words from activity 25 that have the *igh* letter join.

_____

_____

_____

o-e oa

Practise writing each of the words in the box.

close home ode over owe pole coast foam goat load oak soap

Think about this!

Say each word aloud as you write it.
Remember to Look, Say, Cover,
Write and Check!
When you have finished, write each word
three more times on another sheet of paper.

Word practice

old

Practise writing each of the words in the box.

bold bolder cold colder fold folder
hold holder old older sold told

Think about this! ...

Say each word aloud as you write it.
Remember to Look, Say, Cover,
Write and Check!
When you have finished, write each word
three more times on another sheet of paper.

_____

_____

_____

_____

_____

_____

_____

_____

_____

_____

_____

_____

ow ou ough

Practise writing each of the words in the box.

bow flow show slow window boulder
mould shoulder soul dough though

Think about this! Say each word aloud as you write it.
Remember to Look, Say, Cover,
Write and Check!
When you have finished, write each word
three more times on another sheet of paper.

31 Word practice

oo ew

Practise writing each of the words in the box.

*boot cool moon school zoo zoom
crew few mew new stew view*

Think about this! ...

Say each word aloud as you write it.
Remember to Look, Say, Cover,
Write and Check!
When you have finished, write each word
three more times on another sheet of paper.

_____

_____

_____

_____

_____

_____

_____

_____

_____

oa old ou oo

Practise writing all of the words from activity 28 that have the *oa* letter join.

_____

_____

_____

_____

Practise writing all of the words from activity 29 that have the *old* letter join.

_____

_____

_____

_____

_____

Practise writing all of the words from activity 30 that have the *ou* letter join.

_____

_____

Practise writing all of the words from activity 31 that have the *oo* letter join

_____

_____

_____

u-e ue

Practise writing each of the words in the box.

> cute huge June rule tube use cue
> clue due glue queue true

Think about this! ...
Say each word aloud as you write it.
Remember to Look, Say, Cover,
Write and Check!
When you have finished, write each word
three more times on another sheet of paper.

34 Word practice

u ou ui

Practise writing each of the words in the box.

*future humid stupid usual ghoul group
toucan youth bruise cruise sluice suit*

Think about this! Say each word aloud as you write it. Remember to Look, Say, Cover, Write and Check!
When you have finished, write each word three more times on another sheet of paper.

ar or er

Practise writing each of the words in the box.

> bark card farm market corn fork forty
> stork drummer herd porter waiter

Think about this! ...
Say each word aloud as you write it.
Remember to Look, Say, Cover,
Write and Check!
When you have finished, write each word
three more times on another sheet of paper.

36 Practice page 4

ue ou ar er

Practise writing all of the words from activity 33 that have the *ue* letter join.

_____

_____

_____

Practise writing all of the words from activity 34 that have the *ou* letter join.

_____

_____

Practise writing all of the words from activity 35 that have the *ar* letter join.

_____

_____

Practise writing all of the words from activity 35 that have the *er* letter join.

_____

_____

_____

37

37 Compound words

A compound word is made up of two or more existing words.
Practise writing these compound words.
Draw a line between the first and second parts
in each of the examples in the box.

*afternoon carpet greenhouse
playground schoolbag seaside
seesaw snowman sunflower*

un dis

Write each word in the box, then make a new
word by adding a prefix and write it alongside.
Which two words can take both prefixes?

do happy locked tie able grace
honest like

Practise these letter joins

Write the words in the box, looking carefully at how the letters *v* and *w* join the letter *i*.

> *vicar victim villa village visit wicked*
> *widow wiggle willow window wisdom*

Write the words in the box twice. Draw a line to divide the syllables in each word.

> able unable table tablet spoonful fuller
> bullet follow hotter hotpot rotten grotty

41 Handwriting check 2

Write this poem in your best handwriting.

Goodnight, sleep tight.
Don't let the bedbugs bite.
If they do, get your shoe
And hit them till they're black and blue.

Handwriting check 3:
"My Dog"

Write this poem in your best handwriting.

My dog is such a gentle soul,
Although he's big it's true.
He brings the paper in his mouth.
He brings the postman too.

Max Fatchen

Practise writing the words in the box.
Continue your work on another sheet of paper.

about after again an another as
back ball be because bed been
boy brother but by called came
cannot can't could did dig
do not don't door first from

(44) High-frequency words

Practise writing the words in the box.
Continue your work on another sheet of paper.

> girl good got had half has have
> help her here him his home
> house how if jump just last laugh
> little live love made make man many
> may more much must

Practise writing the words in the box.
Continue your work on another sheet of paper.

name new next night not now
off old once one or our out
over people pull push put
ran saw school seen should
sister so some

Practise writing the words in the box.
Continue your work on another sheet of paper.

take than that their them then
there these three time too took
tree two us very want water
way were what who will with
would your

Handwriting check 4:
"The Chair"

Write this poem in your best handwriting.

A funny thing about a Chair:
You hardly ever think it's there.
To know a Chair is really it,
You sometimes have to go and sit.

Theodore Roethke